AT BREAK OF DAY

Written by

Nikki Grimes

Illustrated by

Paul Morin

EERDMANS BOOKS FOR YOUNG READERS

GRAND RAPIDS, MICHIGAN   CAMBRIDGE, U. K.

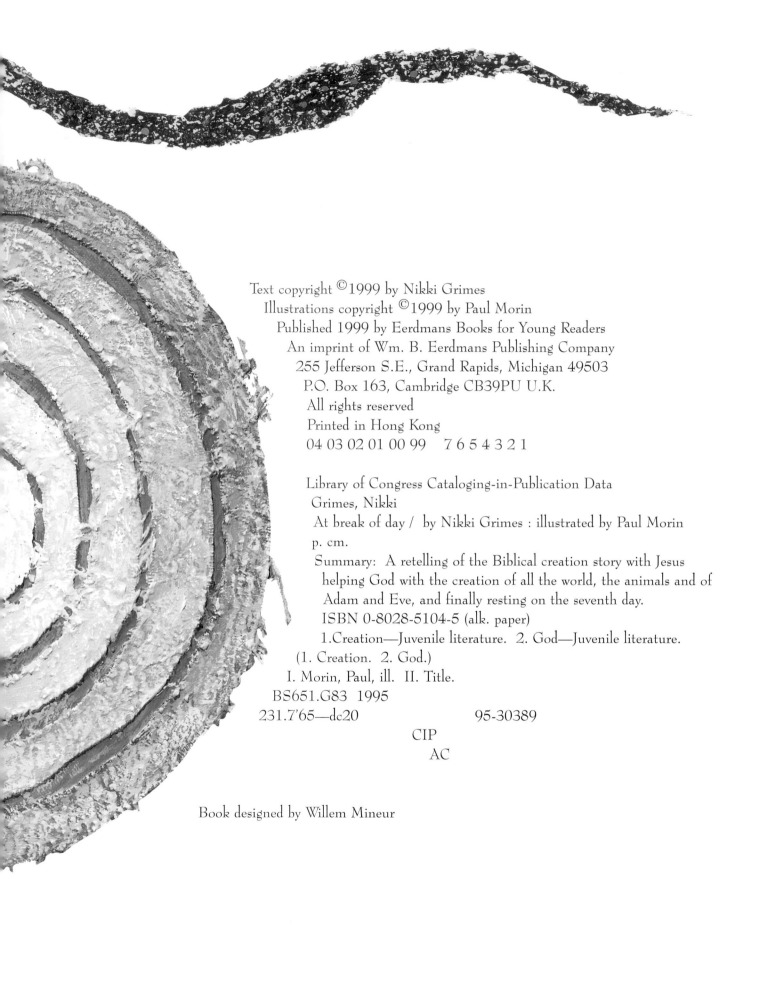

Published 1999 by Eerdmans Books for Young Readers
An imprint of Wm. B. Eerdmans Publishing Company
255 Jefferson S.E., Grand Rapids, Michigan 49503
P.O. Box 163, Cambridge CB39PU U.K.
Printed in Hong Kong
04 03 02 01 00 99   7 6 5 4 3 2 1

Library of Congress Cataloging-in-Publication Data
Grimes, Nikki
 At break of day / by Nikki Grimes : illustrated by Paul Morin
p. cm.
 Summary: A retelling of the Biblical creation story with Jesus
   helping God with the creation of all the world, the animals and of
   Adam and Eve, and finally resting on the seventh day.
 ISBN 0-8028-5104-5 (alk. paper)
 1.Creation—Juvenile literature. 2. God—Juvenile literature.
(1. Creation. 2. God.)
 I. Morin, Paul, ill. II. Title.
BS651.G83 1995
231.7'65—dc20   95-30389
                            CIP
                             AC

Book designed by Willem Mineur

For Rev. Noah Grimes, my grandfather,
who walked the path before me,
and for Jesus Christ, the one true Son.
— N. G.

To Palmer, our little angel,
and to Edmondo and the Piaroa
for walking the golden way.
— P. M.

Once upon a time there
was no time. There was no earth,
or sky, or sea. There was only
darkness and the waters of the deep
and a father and son who watched over them.

The son, knowing exactly what was in his father's
heart, asked, "Now, Father?" And the father said,
"Yes, Son. Now." Then the son leaned
over the darkness and softly blew over the waters.
The darkness swirled as though a giant finger
had dipped into it and given it a stir.

And that's how the universe began.

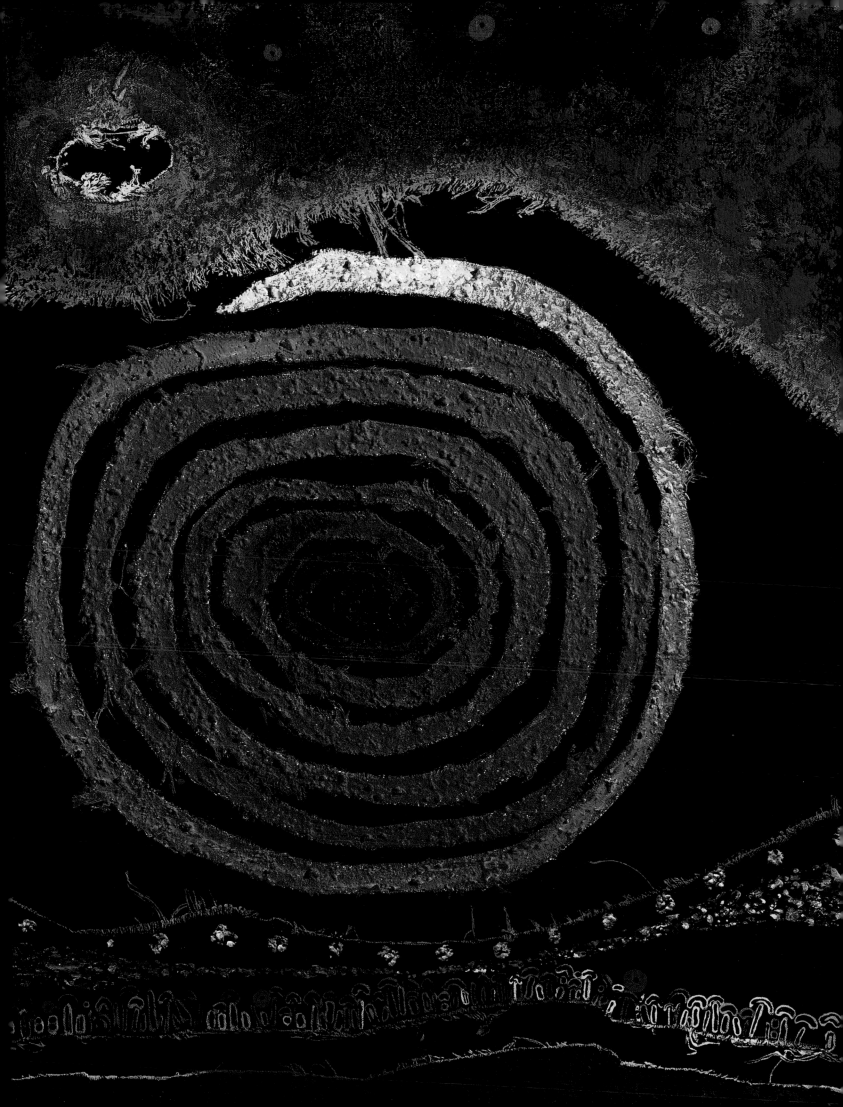

Then the son spoke, and his voice,
as strong as his father's, thundered.
It seemed to come from everywhere
at once, and at the sound of it
the darkness scattered
and made way for light.
And in that light, a myriad
of bright angels appeared.

Then the light was swept
to one side and the darkness
swept to the other side,
as though by a mighty arm.

The father named
the darkness Night
and the light Day.

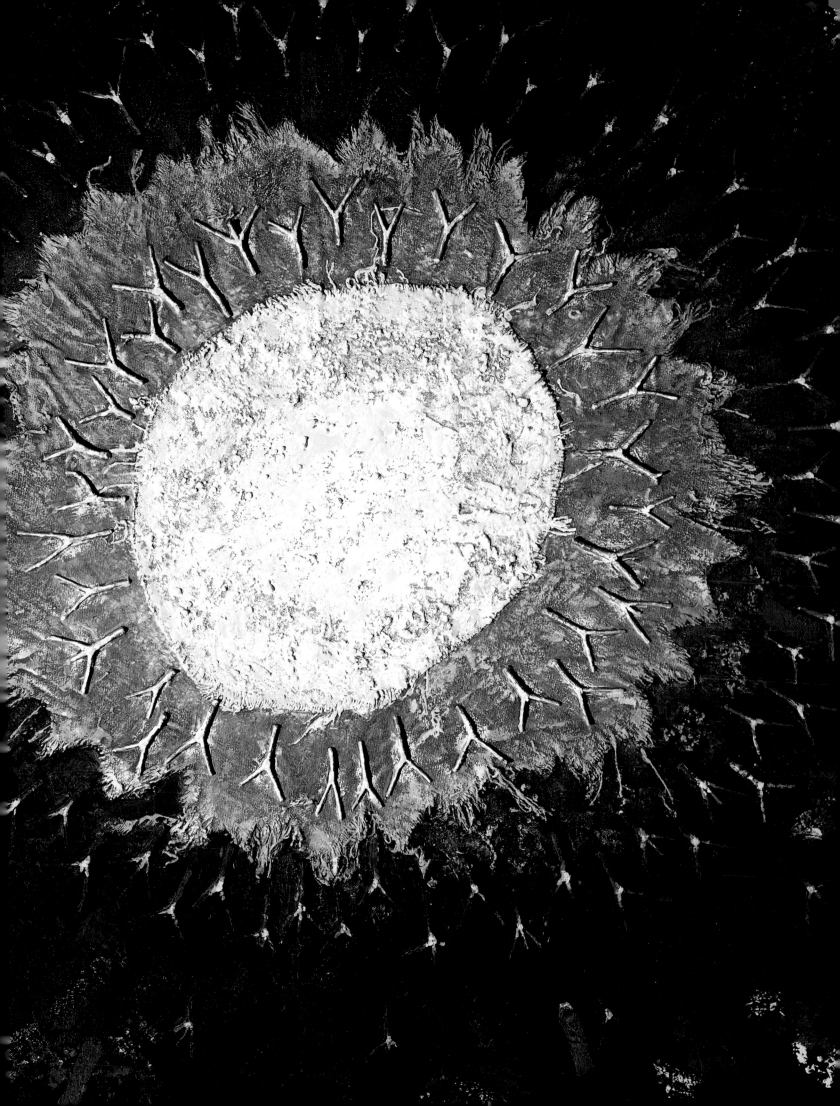

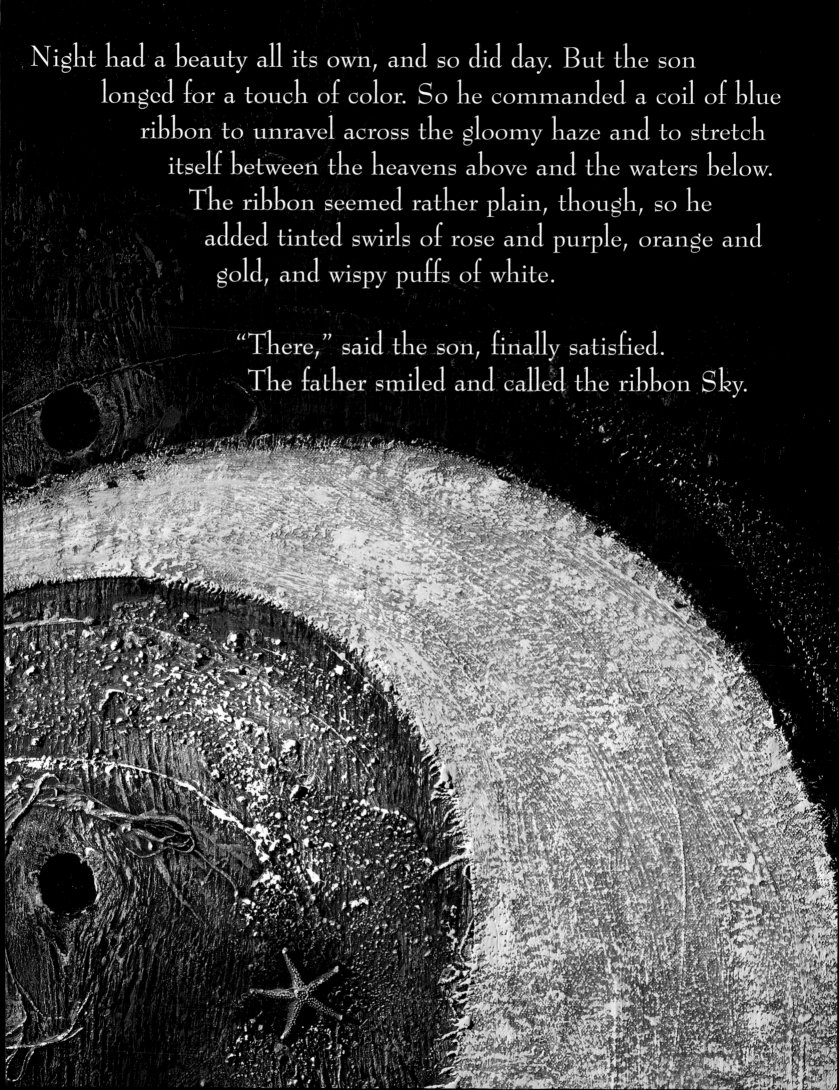

Night had a beauty all its own, and so did day. But the son
longed for a touch of color. So he commanded a coil of blue
ribbon to unravel across the gloomy haze and to stretch
itself between the heavens above and the waters below.
The ribbon seemed rather plain, though, so he
added tinted swirls of rose and purple, orange and
gold, and wispy puffs of white.

"There," said the son, finally satisfied.
The father smiled and called the ribbon Sky.

Early the next morning, the son called out to the waters, "Gather yourselves in one place, and leave space for deserts and plains and foothills and mountains to walk upon." So the waters flowed east and west and north and south, leaving dry places in between. And the father called the dry ground Land. And he called the waters Seas because he liked the sound of it.

The son
noticed that his father
was pleased, so he continued.
"Let there be velvety mosses and
rose-covered meadows, lilacs and long
trailing vines, hyacinths and honeysuckle,
birch and beech, and hearty trees
whose branches are heavy with fruit,"
said the son. "And let each one be full
with its own kind of seeds,
so that there will be growing trees
and plants for many years to come."

And they were.

By now, three days had passed. But the father's plan was still incomplete. So on the fourth day, the son spoke again.

One of his words burst
into a circle of blazing light,
and another spun into a disc of
pale silver.

The father called the blazing circle Sun and
the pale disc Moon, and the son hung them
in the sky to mark the days and the seasons
and the years.

But on what did he hang them?
Only he and his father knew.

"Ahhhh!" sighed the father happily, for the beauty of the sun and the moon delighted him. Seeing his father's pleasure, the son laughed for joy. And the sound of his laughter rose into the sky and shattered into shimmering fragments.

The father called them Stars, and many of them were angels in disguise.

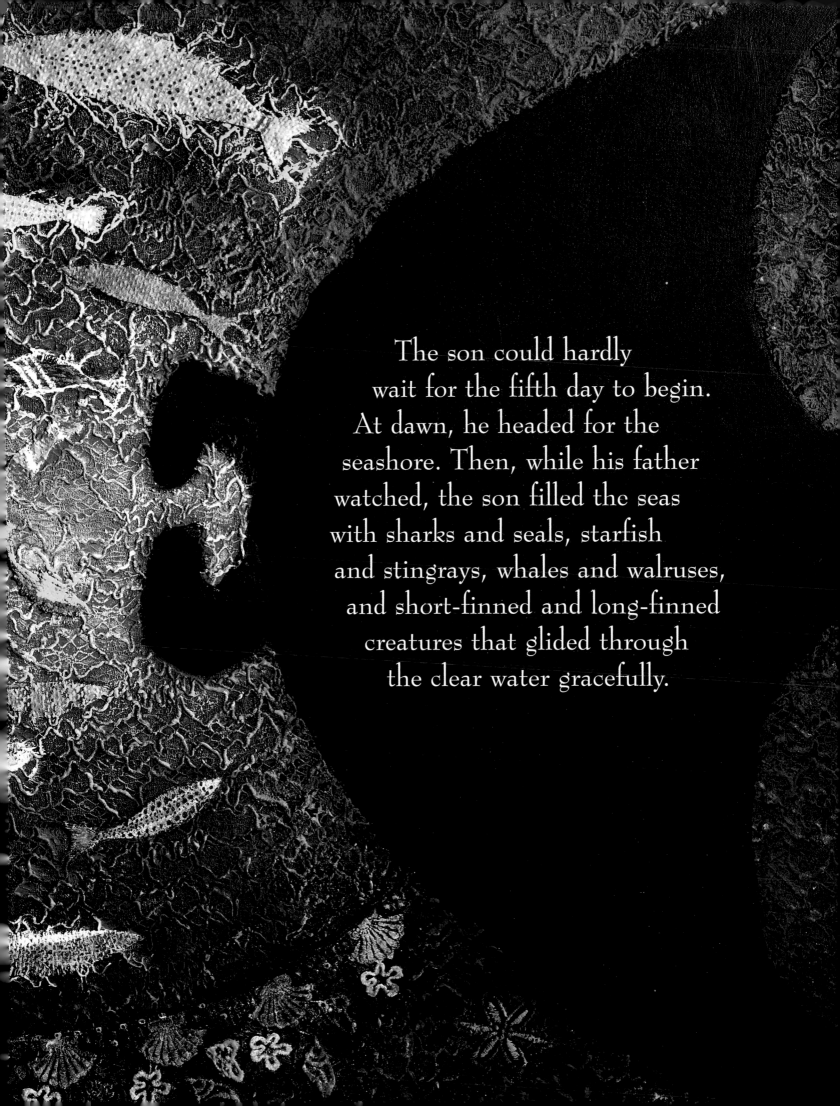

The son could hardly
wait for the fifth day to begin.
At dawn, he headed for the
seashore. Then, while his father
watched, the son filled the seas
with sharks and seals, starfish
and stingrays, whales and walruses,
and short-finned and long-finned
creatures that glided through
the clear water gracefully.

The
father
nodded
his approval.
Then the son
whispered, and the
word he whispered
became a
feather,
and the
feather
traveled on
the warm wind of his breath.

In an instant, the whir of wings
beating the air echoed through field
and forest, and scores of birds soared and
skimmed and swooped across the sky. The
birds looked left and right but could not find the
place where the wind began.

Five days
had come and gone,
and the son had done much to
please his father. Yet, there was more
to do. So on the sixth day the son said,
"Let there be bulls and boars, lions and llamas,
jackals and jaguars, goats and sheep, and creatures
that crawl, and all manner of wild animals
roaring and screeching, loping and leaping,
crouching and creeping upon the earth."

And there were.

The son paused for a moment, gazing at his father. He loved his father, and he enjoyed sharing his feelings and thoughts and visions with him. "Wouldn't it be wonderful to have someone else to share these with?" thought the father. The son, knowing his father's thoughts, nodded.

Aloud, he said, "I'll make someone with a mind and a spirit, who does not wish to be alone. Someone who loves and dreams as we do. I'll make a person. Or, maybe I'll make two."

So the son scooped up a handful of clay, and he molded and shaped a man and a woman. He shaped them with tenderness and care, making them strong and beautiful, with noses that could wrinkle with delight, and eyes through which his love could shine. Then he took a deep breath and blew his life into them.

The father called them Adam and Eve.

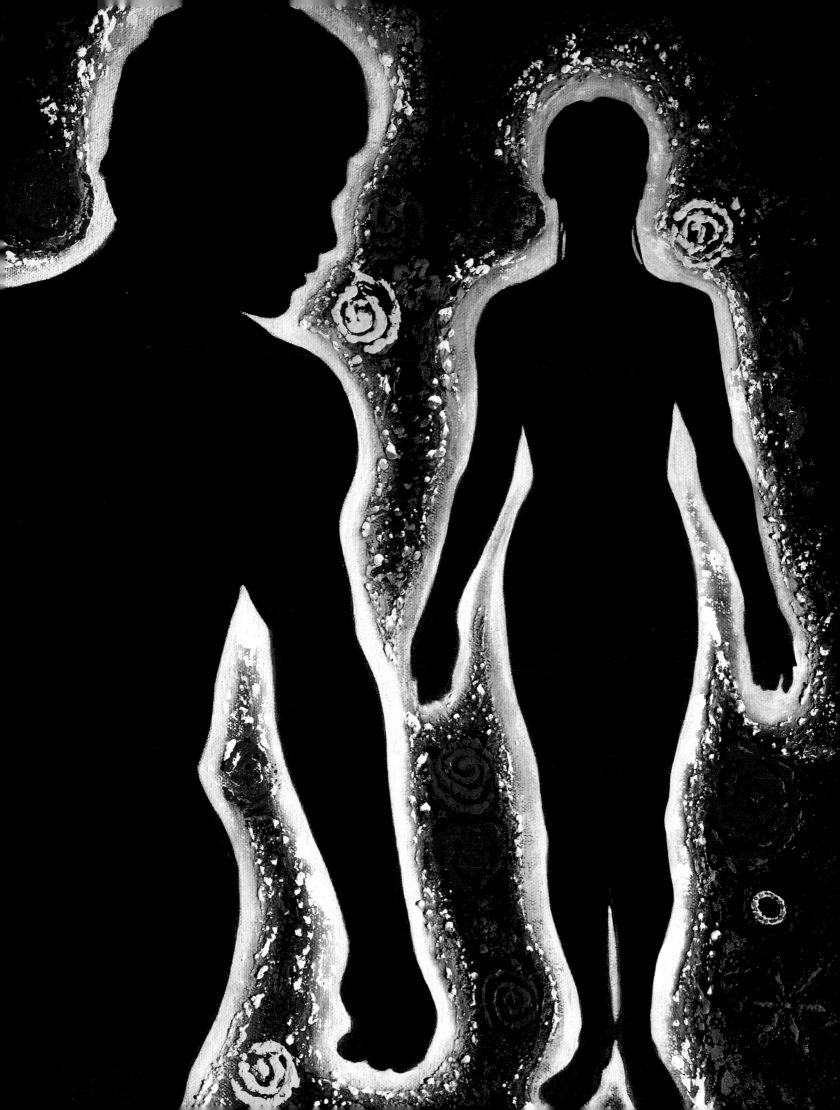

Adam and Eve looked at each other, not quite certain what to do, but the father had already given the son instructions. So the son motioned toward the mighty waters now crashing against the cliffs and toward the birds of the air and the creatures of the land and sea, and he gave all those treasures to Adam and Eve and to all the human beings who would be born after them.

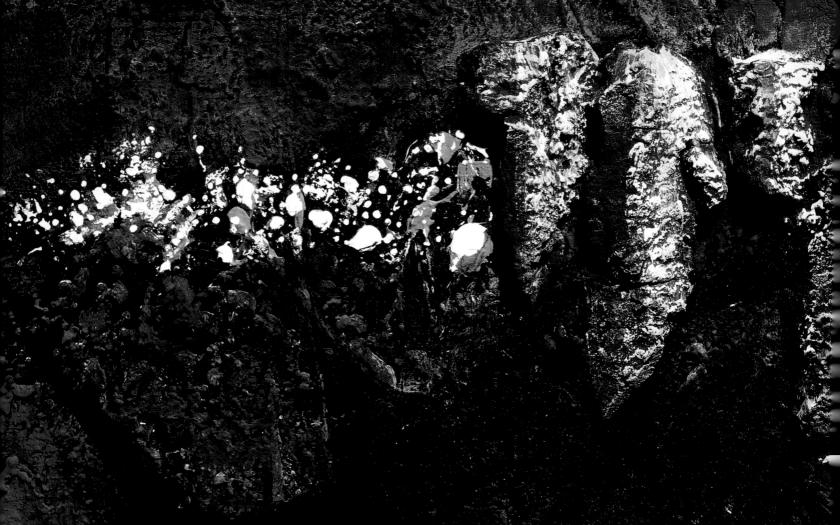

"Take good care of these treasures for me," he said.

The son looked toward the father. "Go on," said the
father, standing in the background. "You're doing fine."

So the son showed Adam and Eve verdant vineyards and
lush orchards and field after field of wild nuts and berries,
wheat and oats, beans and barley, sweet corn and squash,
potatoes and pumpkins.

"Here is enough food for you and all the creatures of the
earth," he said. "Enjoy."

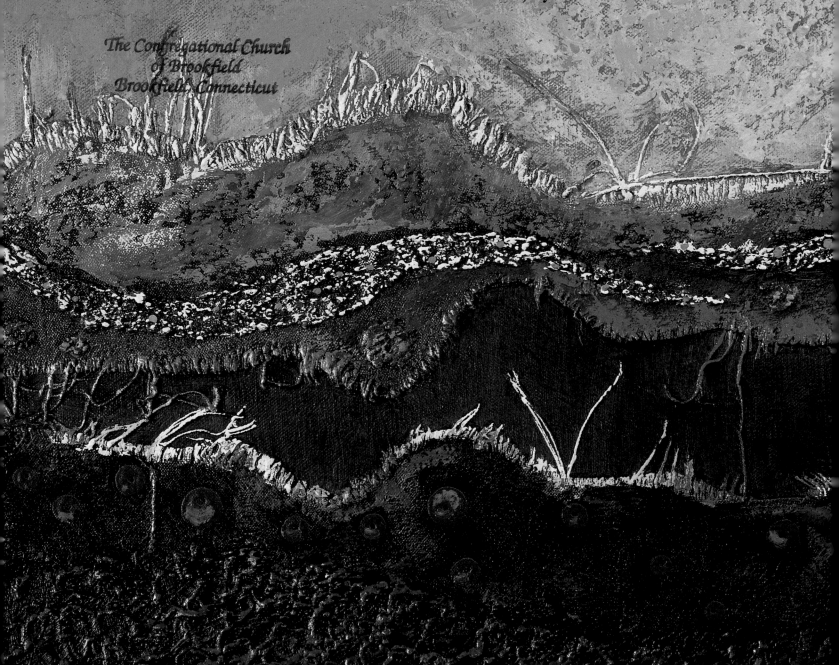

The Congregational Church
of Brookfield
Brookfield, Connecticut

Finally, the son leaned against a mountain
and sighed. He looked at the sky, shot
through with rose and purple light.
And he gazed on the earth, laced
with green growing things, and
on the glistening sea.

Eventually his gaze came to
rest upon the beautiful human
beings he had made, and he
said, "This is good." His
father, standing next to him,
agreed.

And on that day,
the seventh day,
they rested.

Long ago God spoke to our ancestors in many and various ways by the prophets, but in these last days he has spoken to us by a Son, whom he appointed heir of all things, through whom he also created the worlds.

Hebrews 1:1-2